Contents

AGE OF TECHNOLOGY

Are you feeling bored? Maybe you're hanging out by yourself. Perhaps you have friends coming over and you have no idea what to do when they arrive. You're in luck! You live in the age of technology. Computers are everywhere today. You might use one for homework or in the classroom. Mobile phones are equipped with cameras, the internet, music and videos. With just a touch of your fingertips, you can connect to the news, sport and entertainment.

With that much technology around, how can anyone be bored? Now is the time to bust boredom with technology! You can use mobile phones, computers and cameras to create your own newscasts, go on a photo safari or even create a video trailer for your favourite book. Are you ready? Follow the simple instructions, and you and your friends can have a great time while exploring the world of technology.

CAUTION

Remember, safety first! Do not give out any of your personal information online, such as your address or phone number.

BUSTING BOREDOM
WITH TECHNOLOGY

BY TYLER OMOTH

raintree 🍃

a Capstone company — publishers for children

Raintree is an imprint of Capstone Global Library Limited, a company
incorporated in England and Wales having its registered office at 264
Banbury Road, Oxford, OX2 7DY – Registered company number: 6695582

www.raintree.co.uk
myorders@raintree.co.uk

ISBN 978 1 4747 3692 3 (hardback)   ISBN 978 1 4747 3696 1 (paperback)
21 20 19 18 17   22 21 20 19 18
10 9 8 7 6 5 4 3 2 1   10 9 8 7 6 5 4 3 2 1

British Library Cataloguing in Publication Data
A full catalogue record for this book is available from the British Library.

Every effort has been made to contact copyright holders of material reproduced in this
book. Any omissions will be rectified in subsequent printings if notice is given to the
publisher.

All the internet addresses (URLs) given in this book were valid at the time of going to
press. However, due to the dynamic nature of the internet, some addresses may have
changed, or sites may have changed or ceased to exist since publication. While the author
and publisher regret any inconvenience this may cause readers, no responsibility for any
such changes can be accepted by either the author or the publisher

Acknowledgements
Alesha Sullivan, editor; Kyle Grenz, designer; Morgan Walters, media researcher; Katy
LaVigne, production specialist; Marcy Morin and Sarah Schuette, project producers

Photo Credits
Capstone Studio: Karon Dubke, 5, 7, 9, 11, 13, 15, 16, 19, 21, 23, 24, 27, 29; Shutterstock:
Bruno Ismael Silva Alves, (grunge texture) design element throughout, Nevena Radonja,
(gaming controler, camera, video camera) Cover, timurockart, (laptop, keyboard, mouse,
ipod, speakers, phone, microphone) Cover

Printed and bound in India.

MOBILE OVERLOAD

There are over 7.2 billion mobile phones in the world today. That means there are more mobile phones in the world than people!

DIGITAL PHOTO ALBUM

MATERIALS

a digital camera or phone with photo capability

computer or laptop

USB cable

Grab a camera and start snapping photos to create your own *digital* photo album. You can pick any theme, such as animals, different types of plants or flowers or your favourite places around town. Or just take pictures of anything you want! You'll have a digital photo album filled with great shots that you can share with friends and family.

TIP:
Before taking a person's picture, first ask them for their permission.

1 Ask an adult's permission to use a camera or a mobile phone with photo capability. If you don't know how to use the camera or phone, ask for instructions.

2 Decide the theme of the digital album. Is your family going on a trip? Do you want to get action shots of your football team? Your photo album can be anything you want!

3 Start snapping pictures!

4 Connect your camera or phone to a computer using the USB cable.

5 Load the photos onto the computer or laptop. Create an album, a slide show or a screensaver from your new pictures using a basic program on your computer, such as Microsoft Photos or iPhoto.

digital involving or relating to the use of computer technology

USB cable cable used to connect an electronic device to a computer; stands for Universal Serial Bus cable

BE A BLOGGER

MATERIALS

computer with
internet access

Do you love football? Are you a film *fanatic*? Blog about it! Blogging means writing online about a topic that you like. It's a fun way to brush up on your writing skills while sharing your opinion about your favourite things.

TIP:
Create a fun name for your blog that lets people know who you are and what you blog about, such as www.miketalksfootball.com.

1 With a parent or teacher's help, find a safe blogging *domain* online, and sign up.

2 Brainstorm ideas for your topic. Some of the best blogs follow a theme, such as sport, music or cooking.

3 Decide how often you want to post. Do you want to post something every day, once a week or once a month? It's up to you. Whichever you choose, you'll want to stay consistent so your readers know when to look for new posts.

4 Start writing! A blog is sort of like a diary. You don't have to research your topic. You can just say what you think.

TIP:
You can add photos to your blog to make it even more interesting for your readers.

fanatic someone who is wildly enthusiastic about a belief, a cause or an interest

domain subgroup on the internet with website addresses sharing a common suffix or under the control of a particular organization or individual

SHARPEN YOUR SKILLS

When you are writing blog posts, remember to keep your writing fun and readable. Good writing tells a story, keeps the reader interested and uses proper spelling and grammar. Try to use some short sentences and some longer sentences to mix it up.

FILMMAKING 101

MATERIALS

a video camera
or mobile phone
with video
capability

pen and paper

a few friends or
family members

costumes and
props (optional)

computer

USB cable

Do you have a great idea for a film? You could create an exciting action hero film or a *documentary* about something you enjoy. Spook your friends and family with a horror film. Lights! Camera! Action!

1 Ask an adult's permission to use a video camera or a mobile phone with video capability. If you don't know how to use the video camera or phone, ask for instructions.

2 Write a *script*. Every film needs a script that tells the story and describes what the actors say and do. Be as detailed as possible so your story comes to life.

3 Assign cast roles. Get friends or family together, and give everyone a character to play. Each character should dress up in their assigned costume, if they're willing! Don't forget, you'll need a *director* and cameraperson too.

4 Turn on the camera, and start shooting the film.

documentary film or television programme about real situations and people

script story for a play, film or television programme

director person in charge of making a play, film or radio or television programme

5 Connect the camera or phone to a computer using the USB cable. Transfer the video file onto the computer.

6 Edit the film using a basic video editor, such as Windows Movie Maker or iMovie. Ask for an adult's help to learn the basics of the editing program.

7 Gather the cast together to watch the world premiere of your film. Popcorn is optional!

CREATE A NEWSCAST

MATERIALS

a video camera or mobile phone with video capability

pen and paper

computer

USB cable

There's a thunderstorm heading your way. The local rugby team just had a major win. There's breaking news, and you can report it! Remember, news is something that's happening right now. With the help of your friends or family, you could have a whole news team – news, weather and sports.

TIP:

You can play the part by dressing in a suit and tie or a nice dress.

1 Ask an adult's permission to use a video camera or a mobile phone with video capability. If you don't know how to use the video camera or phone, ask for instructions.

2 Decide what kind of news you want to report. Is it a big breaking story? A big sports event? Maybe you want to do a *human-interest piece*. Decide what you like and research the topic.

3 Write the news report. Remember to include important facts about the event.

4 Turn on the camera, and give the news! You can have someone hold the camera or you can set it up on a table.

human-interest piece feature story that discusses a person in an emotional way; a human-interest story presents people and their problems, concerns or achievements in a way that creates viewer interest or sympathy

WRITING A NEWS REPORT

Your audience needs to know the facts about the news and how they might be affected. Related stories or important background information can help. You can also include emotional pieces to really connect to your viewers. To write a gripping news report, it's important to include the following:

- a good introduction to grab the audience's attention
- facts, such as the who, what, when, where, why and how of the news event
- lots of action verbs, such as *create*, *engage* or *defy*
- simple language

5 Using the USB cable, connect your camera to the computer to upload your newscast.

6 Share the news with friends and family!

PRODUCE A BOOK TRAILER

MATERIALS

a favourite book

pen and paper

a video camera or mobile phone with video capability

computer

USB cable

Film *trailers* show new films that will be coming to cinemas. Why not make a trailer for your favourite book? A book trailer is a video that tries to convince the viewer to read the book by showing what the book is about. Have a blast acting out your favourite scenes to intrigue your viewers. Remember not to give away the ending!

1 Brainstorm what you like best about your favourite book.

2 Write a script for the book trailer. Make your trailer as real as possible. Be sure to include the book title and author and your *rating* of the book. Your goal is to make people want to read the book and find out the ending for themselves.

3 Read the script in front of the camera. You can also act out your favourite scenes from the book to spice things up.

4 When you've finished shooting the video, connect the camera to the computer using the USB cable. Upload the video.

trailer short preview from a film or television programme used to advertise it in advance

rating ranking of something based on quality, standard or performance

5 Edit the film using a basic video editor, such as Windows Movie Maker or iMovie. Ask for an adult's help to learn the basics of the editing program.

6 Share your book trailer with friends and family!

LIVE PODCAST

A podcast is similar to a blog but in an audio format. That means instead of writing out a script, you record yourself talking about whatever topic you'd like. Podcasts can add a spark of inspiration to daily life, keep you updated on political topics and even entertain you, all at the click of a button. It's a great way for people to get information on the go. Get ready to create your very own podcast!

MATERIALS

pen and paper

voice recorder or mobile phone with recording capability

USB cable

computer

1 Podcasts are usually done as a series. Think of a good topic that you'd want to talk about consistently, such as your favourite sports team or TV programme. You'll want to come up with a topic that you'll enjoy podcasting about daily, weekly or monthly.

2 Time to brainstorm about your topic! Take notes using the pen and paper. You can read from a script if you want, but a podcast should sound like you're talking directly to your listeners.

3 Hit the record button on the voice recorder or phone, and start talking about your topic. Keep your podcast short. Three to five minutes is a good start.

4 Using the USB cable, connect your recorder or phone to the computer to upload the podcast.

5 Share your podcast with friends and family. They'll be waiting for the next one!

GIVE THIS A TRY:

Have a friend or sibling join you and debate your topic to make your podcast even more fun!

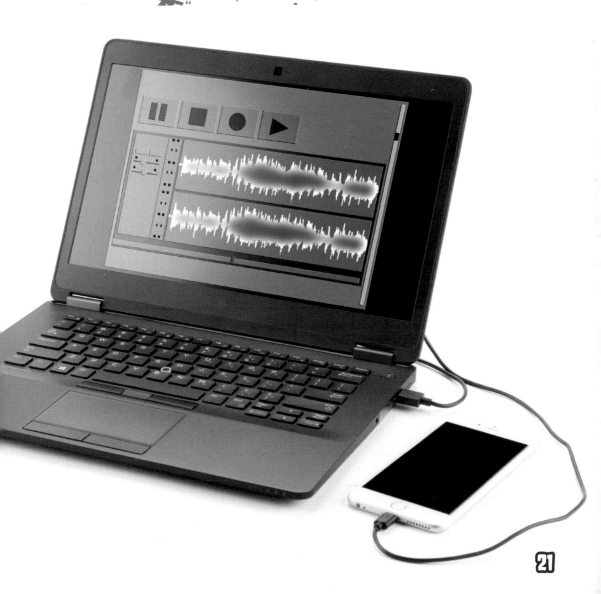

STOP-MOTION FILM

MATERIALS

pen and paper

table or space to use as a stage

action figurines or props

digital camera

tripod (optional)

USB cable

computer

animation software, such as iStopMotion or I Can Animate 2

Stop-motion is a *cinematographic* technique used by filmmakers to make it look like animated figures are moving. Pictures of props or characters are taken quickly, making slight adjustments between each photo. Get ready for a fun, animated adventure using stop-motion photography!

TIP:

Find a quiet place to use for a stage. You don't want a pet or another person touching the stage until your film is done.

1 Brainstorm a story you'd like your film to be about. Use your imagination – your film could be an exciting adventure using action figures or one that shows how to build something. Take notes using the pen and paper.

2 Create a *storyboard* for your film.

3 Set up a stage for your film, such as a tabletop.

cinematography art, process or job of filming

storyboard series of drawings that shows the plot of a television programme or film

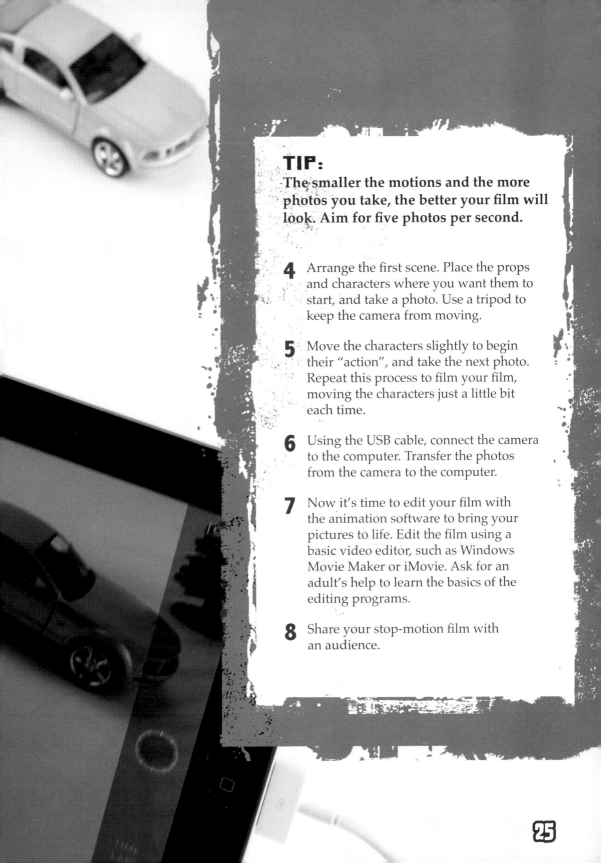

TIP:

The smaller the motions and the more photos you take, the better your film will look. Aim for five photos per second.

4 Arrange the first scene. Place the props and characters where you want them to start, and take a photo. Use a tripod to keep the camera from moving.

5 Move the characters slightly to begin their "action", and take the next photo. Repeat this process to film your film, moving the characters just a little bit each time.

6 Using the USB cable, connect the camera to the computer. Transfer the photos from the camera to the computer.

7 Now it's time to edit your film with the animation software to bring your pictures to life. Edit the film using a basic video editor, such as Windows Movie Maker or iMovie. Ask for an adult's help to learn the basics of the editing programs.

8 Share your stop-motion film with an audience.

CREATE YOUR OWN LOGO

MATERIALS

pen and paper

computer with design software, such as Photoshop or a similar program

TIP:
Too many colours can be distracting, so try and keep your logo simple.

Think of your favourite shops, products or sports teams. They probably all have recognizable logos. A logo is a picture that represents a person or business. Think of some famous logos you recognize, such as the Nike Swoosh, the Golden Arches of McDonald's or even the Batman symbol. What kind of logo would represent you? Get ready to find out!

1 What does it mean to have a good logo? Most of the logos you know and love are simple yet effective. When you see it, you know exactly what it represents. What image would represent you or your business? Brainstorm and take some notes.

2 Choose colours for the logo you want to create.

3 Start sketching. It's easier to draw out your logo first. Figure out what you like best by drawing a few ideas.

4 Open the *graphic design* software on the computer. An adult can help you learn the basics.

graphic design art or skill of combining text and pictures in advertisements, magazines or books

5 Design your logo using the design program. Do you want your logo to represent technology or nature? Maybe something sporty? Keep in mind which colours you want to use. What do you think of when you see blue? Water? The sky? How about red or green? Different colours and combinations can enhance the look and feel of your logo.

6 Show your logo to friends and family.

GIVE THIS A TRY:

Print your logo on iron-on transfer paper, and make a T-shirt with your very own logo on it!

MAKE SOME DIGITAL NOISE

MATERIALS

mobile phone or tablet with access to an app store

If you love music and you have a few minutes to spare, you're in luck. Grab your mobile phone or tablet and make your own songs! It's fun and easy to do, whether you are at home, on the bus or hanging out with friends.

TIP:
The apps Figure and Ninja Jamm are simple music-making apps – and they're free.

1 With an adult's help, download a music-making app onto the mobile phone or tablet.

2 When the app is installed, open it to begin creating music. Once you have the basics figured out, you can personalize your music in many ways. Pick your *rhythm* with the drums. Then add a bass line. Don't forget to add your singing voice too.

3 Share your songs with friends and family, and dance along!

rhythm regular beat in music, poetry or dance

stimulate encourage something to grow or develop

BRAIN WORK

Enjoying and creating music is one of the only activities that *stimulates* your entire brain. It has been proven that music can actually make you smarter and happier. It's like doing press-ups with your mind!

GLOSSARY

cinematography art, process or job of filming

digital involving or relating to the use of computer technology

director person in charge of making a play, film or radio or television programme

documentary film or television programme about real situations and people

domain subgroup on the internet with website addresses sharing a common suffix or under the control of a particular organization or individual

fanatic someone who is wildly enthusiastic about a belief, a cause or an interest

graphic design art or skill of combining text and pictures in advertisements, magazines or books

human-interest piece feature story that discusses a person in an emotional way; a human-interest story presents people and their problems, concerns or achievements in a way that creates viewer interest or sympathy

rating ranking of something based on quality, standard or performance

rhythm regular beat in music, poetry or dance

script story for a play, film or television programme

stimulate encourage something to grow or develop

storyboard series of drawings that shows the plot of a television programme or film

trailer short preview from a film or television programme used to advertise it in advance

USB cable cable used to connect an electronic device to a computer; stands for Universal Serial Bus cable

READ MORE

Computer Coding for Kids, Carol Vorderman (DK, 2014)

Home Lab: Exciting Experiments for Budding Scientists, Robert Winston (DK, 2016)

Technology Activity Book (STEM Starters for Kids), Catherine Bruzzone (B Small Publishing, 2016)

WEBSITES

www.bbc.com/news/technology
Get the latest BBC news on technology, including the web, games, social media and more.

www.sciencechannel.com/science-technology
Learn all about how science and technology shape the world we live in.

INDEX